HANDLING YOUR NEGATIVE EMOTIONS: managing your negative emotions(anger,fear, anxiety)

Table of contents

Chapter one

All you need to know about emotions.

It's crucial to differentiate between what an emotion is and what a feeling is. While the two are related, there's a wider distinction than you seem to assume. It's absolutely something that startled me when I started with my investigation.

Emotions - Emotions are characterized as 'lower level' reactions. They initially arise in the subcortical parts of the brain such as the amygdala and the ventromedial prefrontal cortices. These regions are responsible for creating metabolic responses that have a direct influence on your physical condition. Emotions are inscribed into our DNA and are considered to have evolved as a means to help us adapt swiftly to varied environmental hazards, much like our 'fight response. The amygdala has also been proven to have a role in the production of neurotransmitters that are crucial for memory, which is why emotional memories are typically stronger and simpler to remember.

Emotions have a stronger physical basis than emotions meaning researchers find them simpler to detect scientifically via bodily signs such as blood flow, heart rate, brain activity, facial expressions, and body language.

Feelings - Emotions are considered as preceding feelings, which tend to be our responses to the diverse emotions we encounter. Where emotions may have a more generic experience across all people, feelings are more subjective and are impacted by our particular experiences and perceptions of our reality based on those experiences.

Feelings arise in the neocortical areas of the brain and are the next stage in how we react to our emotions as an individual. Because they are so subjective, they can't be quantified the way emotions can.

Emotions are all those sensations that transform men to impact their judgments, and that is also accompanied by pain or pleasure. Such are rage, sympathy, fear, and the like, with their opposites." Emotion is undoubtedly a broad category that comprises a large range of essential psychological events.

Negative emotions may be regarded as any sensation which causes you to be unpleasant and sad. These feelings make you loathe yourself and others, and lower your confidence and self-esteem, and overall life satisfaction. Emotions that may turn negative include hatred, rage, jealousy, and despair.

Negative emotions are unpleasant and disruptive emotional responses. Examples of negative emotions are sorrow, fear, rage, or jealousy. These sentiments aren't only unpleasant; they also make it hard to operate in your regular everyday life, and they interfere with your capacity to achieve objectives.

It is vital to highlight that no feeling, especially a negative one, is intrinsically harmful. It's totally acceptable to experience these emotions in specific scenarios or situations. These emotions become troublesome when they are persistent and interfere with your capacity to live your life properly.

Chapter two

Types of Negative Emotions

Several unique feelings are often regarded as unpleasant emotions. While such feelings are often a logical reaction to certain events or happenings, they tend to be painful and unpleasant. Some prevalent kinds of unpleasant sensations include:

Anger

Ever had someone told you no to do something you want? How does it make you feel? Does your blood begin to boil, your temperature elevate, and do you metaphorically 'see red'? This is generally how wrath is defined. Your body is reacting to things not going your way, and it's an attempt to try to correct that. Often when we're irritated we'll shout, our expressions will indicate our anger and we may even hurl things around. We're striving to get our own way in a predicament and this is the only approach we can conceive of. If you're consistently reacting to situations in this way, it's a good idea to understand why and come up with more productive approaches.

Anxiety or terror

Fear is often considered as one of the essential basic emotions, and that's because it's intricately tied to our feeling of self-preservation. It's an evolutionary reflex to notify us about unsafe scenarios, unanticipated impediments or failures. We don't experience dread to be anxious, on the contrary, it's there to help us to manage any danger effectively.

Embracing the sense of fear and studying why it occurs could help you prepare yourself proactively to manage events.

Apathy

Like guilt, apathy may be a complex sensation. If you've lost enthusiasm, motivation or interest in the things you've previously liked, this can be tied to apathy. Like wrath, it may occur when we lose control over a setting or occurrence but instead of being outraged, we seek a more passive-aggressive expression of defiance.

Jealousy

Is a emotion of discontent and rage induced by a belief that a loved one may be disloyal. Can also be viewed as a sensation of discontent generated by seeking what someone else owns

Despair

Ever tried to achieve a specific work or target multiple times and not succeeded? Did it make you feel like throwing your hands in the air, and camping out in bed with a huge tub of ice cream for a company? That's despair and it's a sensation that develops when we aren't achieving the results we seek. Despair offers us an excuse to give up on our intended aims and it comes back to a self-preservation attitude. Despair may genuinely be a good reminder to take a break and recuperate, before continuing to pursue a demanding task.

Regret or guilt

Guilt is a tough feeling. We may sense this in relation to ourselves and earlier behaviors that we wish hadn't happened, but also with how our behavior affects individuals around us. Guilt is frequently referred to be a 'moral emotion' and may be another potent stimulant to drive us to make changes in our lives.

Sadness, grief, or loneliness

When you miss a deadline, get a horrible score, or don't acquire the job you had your hopes fixated on, you'll undoubtedly feel melancholy. Sadness happens when we are discontent with ourselves, our achievements or the behavior of someone else around us. Sadness may be nice to experience as it communicates to us we are excited about something. It may be a terrific drive to pursue improvement.

Humiliation\Shame may simply be stated as a dreadful sensation created by awareness of shame, failure, or impropriety

Good news concerning your negative sentiments

Do We Want to Overcome and Stop Negative Emotions Altogether?

In a nutshell, no. It's normal for us to wish to go away from sensations that make us feel miserable. As an evolutionary response, unpleasant feelings in the current world are not truly a signal of a huge threat to us, but mastering and suppressing them fully would be immensely detrimental to us.

Negative emotions are a completely ordinary, healthy and desirable component of living. I think it's vitally crucial not to fall into the 'happiness trap' of believing that these feelings are a sign of weakness or poor emotional intelligence. I know from my experience that striving to hide away from uncomfortable sensations, may lead to greater emotional suffering. As a human being, you will experience a broad array of emotions throughout your lifetime in response to fast-changing situations. No feeling is without meaning. It's when we begin to further investigate and comprehend the rationale behind each sensation, that we find new methods to respond which enhances our emotional growth and sense of wellbeing.

When analyzing negative emotions, it's also vital to recognize that they are not the only source of information you have access to. Before you act upon any emotion you should also endeavor to evaluate your earlier experiences, stored facts and recollections, personal values and planned outcomes for any unique case. Remember That emotion are a low-level reaction thus you get to decide how you respond to them and not let them rule your actions.

How Can They Impact our Health and Wellbeing?

It's not unpleasant emotions that instantly influence our health and wellbeing, but how we react and process them when we do experience them that actually counts. Staying hooked on negative emotions may enhance our bodies' production of our stress hormone, cortisol, which in turn depletes our cognitive ability to problem solve proactively and may also weaken our immune systems, leaving us more prone to various ailments. Chronic stress has also been associated with a decreased lifespan.

Anger is the negative emotion that has been proven to have the largest effect on our health and well-being, particularly if this is badly managed. Studies have related anger to various health conditions including high blood pressure, cardiovascular disease and digestive troubles

Excessive amounts of anger raise levels of cortisol, which were connected with decreased immune system performance. I discovered out that consistently angry folks were more likely to have a cold, the flu, asthmatic symptoms and skin ailments such as rashes compared to non-chronically angry people. A recent branch of research has explored the effect of negative emotions on our sensory perceptions and experiences.

5 Proven Benefits of Negative Emotions

It's not all doom and gloom. When controlled successfully, unpleasant feelings may have proved beneficial for our wellbeing, and much more investigation has been invested into comprehending this component of negative emotions.

I've simplified some of the main conclusions from the research addressing how negative emotions could aid you:

1. Sadness could help you pay closer attention to detail

Where happy emotions signal that everything is well in our immediate surroundings, negative emotions inform us that there are difficulties or new stimuli that need our more focused attention. Sadness sends us the warning that something is not right and asks us to pay our attention to why this may be, what may be causing it, and what we need to do to remedy it.

2. Anger may be a strong incentive to seek mediation

Anger is only followed by hostility in around 10 percent of occurrences. Anger has been demonstrated to inspire you to search after aggressive ways to address occasions or folks you've regarded problematic but doesn't obligatory mean through confrontation or violent activities. Anger is a strong alarm that reminds you to reflect on why someone may be behaving a specific way, and what you can do to restore peace.

3. Anxiety develops new techniques of tackling obstacles and challenges

When we feel nervous, we'll strive to do anything we can not to feel that way anymore. Anxiety is tightly related to our 'fight or flight reflex, which helps your body to accumulate energy rapidly, ready for action. When challenged with risky conditions, fear will take over and push us to seek solutions swiftly in order to prevent danger

4. Guilt helps you alter unwanted behavior

Guilt may be an immensely useful sensation. It's essentially our moral compass and when it goes off, it's a strong warning that we may have done or said something hurtful to someone we care about. It's like our internal method for punishing ourselves after we've done something bad. People who are more prone to feeling guilty are less likely to steal, consume drugs, resort to violence or drink and drive.

5. Jealousy drives you to try harder

Jealousy isn't always unpleasant. Most of the time it's what psychiatrists refer to as 'benign envy'. Benign envy has been proved to drive youngsters to perform better on tests and in academics, as witnessing another student earn a good grade made it more tangible for them to attain too.

Next time you feel envy because someone else has accomplished a desired goal, try to regard this as a good thing - it means the goal is totally attainable for you too.

Learn how to respond versus react

Do you know the difference between how you reply versus how you react? Negative emotions usually push us to react fast to a specific situation. When we feel irritated, we may lash out or shout. When we grow sad, we may withdraw and reject others around us.

Sometimes we need to act on these desires, but frequently we don't. By analyzing your unpleasant feelings you may start to develop your awareness of how you respond, and instead start to switch this to beneficial ways of reacting – which can mean learning that no reaction is required at all.

Know when to take a break

Know when to take a day to yourself. If you are frequently experiencing terrible emotions and striving to manage them, your body is alerting you something isn't right.

Take a day to re-center. Fill your day with happy experiences, doing the things that you know nourish you and make you feel wonderful. This sort of pause may assist to realign your thoughts, giving you some room to reflect on why you might be feeling negative emotions, and come up with some constructive coping skills. This is only a short aggregate of the things I believe would be most useful, but it all comes down to you as an individual. Some of them may function fairly well, while others not so well. Make sure you try out a few different techniques and find the ones that perform best for you.

A Look at Negative Emotions in the Workplace

Our job and the workplace may be sources of enormous happiness and satisfaction for us. On the other side, they may also be a battleground for misery and a range of bad sentiments. These sentiments may be particularly challenging at work as we seek to limit our reactions in front of professional colleagues and our bosses. Failing to do so can result in our workers being on the line. I'm very sure that's something we all want to avoid!

Below I've chosen five of the most usual unpleasant sentiments that come up during work and what they may be signaling:

Anger - Anger at work could emerge for many varied factors. You might be upset with a lethargic employee, a despotic employer, cutbacks or unfair treatment. Of all the unpleasant emotions, wrath is likely the one you most want to keep under control in the workplace. If you feel the familiarity of wrath rising at work, remember to respond and not react. Remove yourself from the scenario by taking a walk and receiving some fresh air. Use mindfulness to bring your body and mind back to a state of calm and manage the situation intelligently.

Dread - In uncertain times dread could show up at work for a few reasons. You might be apprehensive about redundancy or job security. Or you might experience dread and anxiety because of a terrible boss or colleague. Your fear is informing you that you don't feel secure. Problem address what is causing your fear and what measures you need to take care to create beneficial change. If you're nervous about job security, making sure you update your CV and taking a course to enhance your talents, may help you feel secure and in command of your position. When it comes to a toxic colleague or boss, seek aid. Speak to a trustworthy coworker, friend or HR person and receive support.

Guilt - Guilt is a tricky one. Maybe you took a sick day when you shouldn't have or blamed a colleague when you missed a deadline. Guilt is your moral compass informing you something is improper. You can't go back and reverse earlier conduct but you can pay attention when the emotion arrives and strive to make modifications.

Jealousy - Is there one particular colleague who always seems to get the praise? Who may have pipped you for that promotion, pay boost or huge client? Jealousy may come up at work when we perceive someone is accomplishing the aims we wish to obtain ourselves but may be having problems in doing so. It's vital not to let this to become bitter jealousy and remain clear of gossip (unless it's nice) at the water cooler, tempting as it may be. Use your jealousy to motivate you to attain the goals. Instead of being resentful, approach the colleague for advice on how you may be able to improve too. Seek their assistance and you may form an alliance that reaps advantages, instead of a dispute that helps no one.

Apathy - Feeling disinterested in your work position or obligations is a symptom that needs to be explored. If you're feeling disengaged with your job and coworkers, it can be a hint that it's time to move on or seek other challenges. No one enjoys being bored and this can be your passive-aggressive technique of sticking your heels in rather than accepting change when necessary. If this sense of apathy is growing into other sections of your life, it can be a sign of depression, so be sure to obtain professional help if you're finding it hard to feel enthusiastic about life. Just as terrible sentiments outside of work are an indicator that something needs to change, the same is true when they develop at work. Explore the feeling proactively and see where it leads you.

Emotionally intelligent individuals rapidly learn to detect unpleasant emotions and utilize them in adaptable ways to attain better success. The following are six acknowledged advantages connected with negative emotions:

1. GREATER SELF-AWARENESS

Negative emotions provide a protective purpose by alerting us to possible hazards and letting us know when it's time to adjust what we are doing or thinking. Because negative emotions tend to be experienced more intensely, they must be carefully addressed. Emotionally intelligent individuals absorb what they learn from their encounters with unpleasant emotions and utilize that knowledge to develop their self-awareness. This helps them to more correctly recognize what they are experiencing in future scenarios and strategically analyze whether those feelings will best benefit them in that time.

Self-awareness is a critical component of success since it enhances our judgment and helps us recognize chances for professional development and personal progress. Many psychologists argue that the healthiest, most successful leaders are the ones who are most self-aware.

2. MOTIVATED ACTION

Negative emotions such as dread or worry may be potent motivators that inspire endurance. They function by restricting our area of attention and perception to prepare us to behave in certain ways. All humans feel dread, but emotionally intelligent individuals know how to harness their fear and utilize it to their benefit.

All humans feel dread, but emotionally intelligent individuals know how to harness their fear and utilize it to their benefit.

The wise use of fear entails the capacity to notice its existence in the present and relabel it as something valuable. For example, it is typical to feel worried before presenting a presentation at work. People with strong emotional intelligence detect indicators of dread and employ cognitive reappraisal to regulate fear. They may persuade themselves that dread is merely their body's way of providing them the energy they need to produce a fantastic performance. In many circumstances, anxiety may promote performance just as readily as it can debilitate it.

3. GREATER ATTENTION TO DETAIL

According to studies, if you need to evaluate a document for flaws, it may be useful to nurture a little gloomy attitude. Negative emotions have been demonstrated to be useful while engaged in tasks that need more attention to detail. Periods of melancholy foster slower, more methodical cognitive processing. For instance, when individuals feel melancholy, they depend less on rapid judgments and pay more attention to small details that matter. Negative emotions are beneficial for informing us when events are new or hard and when more focus is required to generate an appropriate reaction.

4. ENHANCED CREATIVITY

Negative emotions have been related to better creative production. Researchers have observed that persons feeling annoyance or rage are less likely to think in systematic ways, and more likely to engage in flexible, unstructured mental processes. This form of thinking is related to being able to perceive the "bigger picture," which may be advantageous during brainstorming sessions. Furthermore, since anger generates a more stimulating sense, it might be good for producing the sustained focus required to address issues more creatively.

5. GREATER PROBLEM SOLVING

Anxiety is a valuable feeling when speedy answers to intricate situations are required. Anxiety and panic increase the body's fight-or-flight response, which may assist in problem-solving procedures. The fight-or-flight mechanism permits the body to consume a considerable quantity of energy in a short period. This helps prepare the body to behave rapidly in potentially harmful or unpleasant circumstances. Anger may also be advantageous while attempting to problem-solve since it has been connected to greater performance in negotiations, particularly when they are combative in character.

6. AUTHENTIC PRESENCE

Emotionally intelligent individuals are open-minded when it comes to their emotions. They objectively examine negative feelings, pick the ones that will best help them, put them into practice, and leave the others behind. This permits individuals to maintain a high degree of congruence between their internal sentiments and external displays of emotion and actions. Emotionally intelligent individuals frequently appreciate honesty and, since they are not hesitant to reveal their feelings, are often considered real and true persons.

Chapter Three

Unhealthy Ways of Coping

Unfortunately, individuals frequently resort to unproductive or even dangerous methods of dealing with bad feelings. While they could give immediate relief, they often make issues worse in the long term.

Ignoring Emotions

Ignoring sentiments (such "stuffing your anger") is not the best method to cope with them. Generally speaking, it does not make them vanish, but might instead lead them to come out differently2 (thus, you could shout at your kid while you're genuinely unhappy about a problem at work).
Negative emotions suggest that what you are doing in your life isn't working. So when you ignore them, you can't make any adjustments, and you continue to suffer terrible sensations.

Ruminating on Emotions

Rumination includes lingering on wrath, bitterness, and other negative sentiments. This magnifies unpleasant feelings, but it also carries health repercussions. 3 So it's crucial to listen to your emotions and then take actions to let them go.

Withdrawal or Avoidance

When something is stressful, you could find yourself attempting to avoid it so that you don't have to feel those negative emotions. If a person or scenario gives you anxiety, for example, you could take measures to avoid such triggers. The difficulty is that avoidance coping makes unpleasant feelings worse in the long term.

Destructive or Risky Behaviors

If you don't deal with the emotions you are experiencing, they might create difficulties with physical and emotional health. This is especially true if you depend on dangerous activities such as drug use or self-harm to deal with stressful feelings.

How to handle Negative Emotions

Fortunately, there are more beneficial methods to cope with challenging emotions. These tactics may help you manage while also strengthening your capacity to control your emotions.

Understand Your Emotions

Look inside and find the events producing tension and unpleasant emotions in your life. Looking at the cause of the sensation and your response might reveal significant information. Negative feelings might emerge from a triggering event, such as an onerous task. Your thoughts around an incident also play a role. The way that you perceive what occurred might influence how you experience the incident and whether or not it produces tension.

Change What You Can

Once you better understand your emotions and what is producing them, you may start taking measures to solve the situation. Minimizing or removing some of your stress triggers may help you experience unpleasant emotions less often. Some methods that you could do this include; Cutting down on work stress, frequently by delegating responsibilities, creating boundaries, and Research has shown that strategies like repressing your emotions are useless and can even be detrimental.

So instead of attempting to ignore your feelings, finding strategies to understand, embrace, and reinterpret your emotions is frequently more useful. Negative feelings are common and even anticipated. The idea isn't to suppress these sensations but to create better methods of controlling them. Building these coping skills may lead to improved emotional resilience and well-being.

Seeking help.

Learning the techniques of assertive communication to address relationship difficulties. Changing unfavorable mental patterns using a technique known as cognitive restructuring. Not every cause of stress can be modified or removed. It is crucial to avoid worrying over what you can't alter and focus on what's within your power. Making adjustments in your life may cut down on unpleasant feelings, but it won't eradicate your stress triggers. As you make adjustments in your life to bring about less irritation. you will also need to discover healthy outlets for coping with these feelings. Regular exercise may give an emotional boost and an outlet for negative emotions, Meditation can help you discover some inner space to deal with so your emotions don't seem overpowering. Finding chances for having fun and obtaining more laughter in your life may help shift your outlook and reduce stress. Remember that everyone's demands and talents are different. The trick is typically to try a few alternative approaches to determine what works for you and your scenario. Once you have identified ways that are perfect for you, you'll feel less overwhelmed when unpleasant feelings come.

Accept Your Emotions

Learning to accept unpleasant emotions is also a useful technique of handling these challenging sentiments. Acceptance implies understanding that we are feeling fearful, angry, sad, or irritated. Instead than attempting to ignore or repress these sensations, you allow them to exist without concentrating on them.

More on handling Your Negative Emotions

Techniques for Managing Negative Emotions

The discipline of positive psychology is seeing a "second wave" of study that is focused not just on what makes us happy, resilient, and able to flourish but also on the dark side of happiness.

5 Experts have learned more about how our negative emotions influence us and what to do with them, and how we may stay emotionally healthy throughout the process.

Just as there are advantages to negative emotions, there are detriments to "false positivity" when we punish ourselves for feeling these natural states and attempt to ignore them or push ourselves to pretend we feel more positive than we do.

Tears

T - Teach and learn: This means embracing self-awareness and enhancing your understanding of your body and mind, and how they are reacting to stress and other emotional states. This helps you to understand when you are disturbed and why, and be better able to comprehend the messages your body is expressing.

E - Express and empower sensory and embodied experiences: This one seems a bit more difficult but it just includes fostering openness and curiosity inside yourself to strengthen your acceptance of what arises.

A - Accept and befriend: It may be incredibly good to deliberately work on strengthening your self-compassion and tolerance for annoyance.

R - Re-appraise and re-frame: You may utilize cognitive behavioral techniques to perceive things differently.

S - Social support: This might incorporate the practice of loving-kindness meditation, which can enhance your emotions of connectedness to others and your self-compassion while you engage in relationships.

Hope

H - Hedonic well-being and happiness: Research shows that it can be highly beneficial to have a 3-to-1 ratio of positive vs. negative emotions, meaning that you add positive experiences to your life, focus on happy memories and savor successes, for example, to increase the amount of time you spend authentically feeling good.

O - Observe and attend to Try to cultivate mindfulness and non-judgmentally attention to things in life.

P - Physiology and behavioral changes: Focus on relaxation, breathing exercises, and self-care.

E - Eudaimonia: Strive for objectives in life and a feeling of sincerity.

The notion of "controlling" unpleasant emotions is a tricky one. It doesn't mean avoiding them—avoidance coping is a sort of coping that strives to achieve this, and it may frequently backfire.

1 . It also doesn't mean allowing these negative feelings to wreak havoc on your life, your relationships, and your stress levels. Unmanaged anger, for example, may push us to ruin relationships if we let it.

Managing negative emotions is more about acknowledging the fact that we are experiencing them, discovering why we are feeling this way, and allowing ourselves to hear the lessons that they are bringing us before we release them and go ahead.

Yes, that remark may seem a bit unusual, but our emotions are undoubtedly created to be messengers to tell us something. These signals may be quite beneficial if we listen.

Managing negative emotions also entails not allowing them to overpower us. We can keep things under control without denying that we are experiencing them. When we speak about so-called negative emotions, it's crucial to understand that these feelings, in and of themselves, aren't negative as in "bad." It is more than they are in the area of negativity as compared to optimism.

2. Emotions aren't always good or evil, they are only states and signals that help us to pay greater attention to the circumstances that cause them. This may either encourage us to generate more of a given experience or less, for example.

Unlike other emotions, negative feelings are not necessarily pleasant to experience. But, like other feelings, they exist for a purpose and may be rather valuable to experience.

How Do Negative Emotions Affect Us?

Anger, fear, resentment, frustration, and anxiety are unpleasant emotional states that many individuals feel often but want to avoid. And this is understandable—they are meant to make us uncomfortable.

Negative Emotions Can Cause Stress

These unpleasant emotional states might produce additional stress in your body and your thinking. This is unpleasant but also may lead to health risks if the stress becomes persistent or overpowering.

3. Nobody wants to feel uncomfortable, therefore it is normal to desire to escape these sensations, and the hazards of mismanaged stress are real. However, there is a notion that individuals sometimes have that these emotions will stay forever or that the feelings themselves are the issue.

Negative Emotions Also Provide Information. More frequently, these sentiments are useful since they may also convey signals. For example, Anger and worry suggest that something has to change and that possibly our well-being has been compromised.

Fear is a request to raise your degree of safety.

Frustration or resentment leads us to modify something in a relationship.

Unpleasant emotions are there to inform us that something needs to change and to push us to accomplish that change.

Even Positive Emotions Have Downsides

Positive psychologists also contend that although there are numerous advantages to positive emotional states like optimism, pleasure, and appreciation, there are also negative impacts that may emerge from them. Optimism, for example, has been related to several favorable consequences for health and happiness as well as a personal accomplishment.

4. Unchecked optimism, however, may lead to unreasonable expectations and even unsafe risks that can lead to loss and all of the unpleasant emotions that might come with it. Greater difficult emotional states like worry, however, might lead to the drive to make adjustments that can bring more success and prevent danger.

Negative emotions are designed to keep us safe and to motivate us to improve our lives, just as positive emotions are. Why Toxic Positivity Can Be So Harmful

A better method is to accept and even enjoy our negative feelings, while simultaneously participating in activities that might honestly counter-balance these unpleasant emotions.

Various tactics are advocated as ways to improve positive emotional states and personal resistance to stress and emotions of negativity so that negative emotional states don't seem as overpowering. Because of the studies on optimism, we know that this may be a helpful thing in itself. Here are some other tactics that may be utilized to manage unpleasant feelings.

Best Possible Self Exercise

This requires envisioning—you guessed it—your ideal potential self and what that might look like. This activity has been demonstrated to raise the mood and create a feeling of optimism, both of which generate lasting effects.

5. This practice may be done as a journaling activity or just a visualization method, but essentially entails visualizing your life in the future and pushing yourself to envisage the greatest possible life you can live, the best possible version of yourself that you can be. Research has revealed that persons who

participate in picturing their greatest self for five minutes a day for two weeks enjoy a higher pleasant mood and an increase in optimism compared to those who spent the same amount of time just thinking about activities in their day. For five minutes a day, this is a terrific use of time.

Gratitude Letter or Visit

This practice includes expressing thanks to persons who have done good things for you. This includes both minor and major acts of kindness.

6. This may be a note to an elementary school teacher who motivated you to achieve your best or a visit to a neighbor to let them know how much you enjoy knowing they are there. It may be any letter or personal journey and discussion conveying to someone what they have done for you, what it has meant to you, and that you appreciate them.

A Word From Verywell

Even though you prefer to have a cheerful viewpoint, bad feelings will come. Knowing how to handle these emotions might help you feel better in the now and the future.

www.ingramcontent.com/pod-product-compliance
Lightning Source LLC
LaVergne TN
LVHW080819170826
845678LV00011B/2080
* 9 7 9 8 3 5 2 4 2 6 3 1 9 *